C000027653

RETROACTIVE JEALOUSY

A Guide To Transforming Your Pain Into Power

RYDER WINCHESTER

CONTENTS

DOWNLOAD THE AUDIO VERSION OF THIS BOOK FREE

This book is best enjoyed in its audio format. If you love listening to audio books on-the-go, I have great news for you. You can download the audio book version of this book for **FREE** just by signing up for a **FREE** 30-day audible trial! See below for more details!

Audible trial benefits

As an audible customer, you'll receive the below benefits with your 30-day free trial:

- Free audible copy of this book
- After the trial, you will get 1 credit each month to use on any audiobook
- Your credits automatically roll over to the next month if you don't use them

- Choose from over 400,000 titles
- Listen anywhere with the audible app across multiple devices
- Make easy, no hassle exchanges of any audiobook you don't love
- Keep your audiobooks forever, even if you cancel your membership
- And much more

Click the links below to get started:

For Audible US:
bit.ly/retroactivejealousylisten

For Audible UK:
bit.ly/retroactivejealousylistenuk

INTRODUCTION

If you are reading this book then congratulations! You have decided you are ready for change. You are ready to become empowered and ready to get your life back into your control. This book is a completely transparent, in-depth and detailed account of my journey through retroactive jealousy, from its vulnerable innocent origins, to its ultimate epic defeat. This book is also a comprehensive guide on how I personally struggled with and eventually transformed the insidious beast into personal strength and power. At the risk of offending you the reader and retroactive jealousy sufferer, I bring you this piece of truth; Retroactive jealousy was one of the greatest things to ever happen to me. That thought may seem impossible to you at this stage. It may even anger you. But you will likely one day feel a deep sense of gratitude that you suffered through this pain once you have undergone enough of a positive transformation. My Retroactive Jealousy's healing and defeat was a physical, spiritual and mental evolution. Although its grasp caused much pain, heartbreak and despair, victory over it blossomed a more loving, strong, patient, thoughtful and confident version of myself. I was reborn anew in the ashes of Retroactive jealousy's defeat and spread my wings into a brighter future that would not have been known to me had I not suffered the way I had suffered.

WHAT IS RETROACTIVE JEALOUSY

If you have picked up this book then you likely do not need an explanation of Retroactive Jealousy. But a description of its symptoms and traits from an external being may make you feel less alone, as you have likely felt isolated in your pain in the past. Your partner, friends, and family members may be wholly confused by your affliction, leaving you further in despair. But you are not alone. There are thousands of sufferers (and ex-sufferers) all around the world that feel this pain just like you. Retroactive Jealousy is the seemingly uncontrollable obsession and curiosity regarding your partner's sexual and relationship history. This obsession often causes sufferers to become encapsulated in a trance-like state of anxiety, wherein they feel the need to extract any discover any information and details of their partner's past. These attempts at extracting information can often lead to much drama and tempestuous upsets in relationships. The obsessive thoughts associated with Retroactive Jealousy can be likened to the symptoms of obsessive-compulsive disorder. The sufferer's mind regularly enters loops of intrusive painful thoughts, usually involving a past interaction their partner had with an ex-lover. These intrusive thoughts are mostly illusory and imagined as the sufferer conjures up their mental image of these past encounters. Often the sufferers partner may mention a small detail in passing and the sufferer will take this tiny detail and either use it to slyly draw out more information from their partner, or use it as a puzzle piece to create a larger imaginary image in their head of what they thought could have happened in their partners past. These assumed or imagined past happenings are not usually based on the reality of what happened. These intrusive thoughts and seemingly uncontrollable actions are accompanied and fueled by deeply painful emotions.

BEFORE WE BEGIN

There are a few important points to make before you begin your journey of healing. Firstly, to speed your journey up, I will refer to Retroactive Jealousy as 'RJ' for the remainder of this book. Secondly, I have made an effort not to go into any details that may trigger you the reader and RJ sufferer. But as you know all so well, triggers have a life of their own and will appear as they please. We will look in-depth at triggers later on in our path. Should you feel triggered at any point then please follow some of the exercises found later in the book. Remember, if you can't feel it then you cannot heal it. As painful as triggers are, they are one of the secrets to healing! They are little hidden (painful) gems of growth and personal power when dealt with strategically and with conscious presence. So from here on out, if you are triggered then see it as a good thing! It's an opportunity to use the trigger to your advantage to grow. Thirdly, you may have heard that it is impossible to completely rid yourself of RJ and you may still be triggered from time to time. This may be true for some ex-sufferers, but it's still a marvelous improvement in the individual's life. I would like you, the reader to guess how much of my RJ remains. 0%! I am absolutely 100% cured of my RJ and I am never, ever triggered. I cannot promise this for you the reader as everyone is unique and will experience growth differently. But you must know and realize deeply that absolute healing has been accomplished and can be possible for you. Lastly and most importantly, you must decide **here and now** that you have had enough of this life-denying pain and you are ready to stop projecting your pain out on to your partner, friends, and family. Making the brave, empowering decision to overcome your RJ will enrich your life beyond your current comprehension. It will relieve your friends and family's lives of your RJ's negative outward projections. It will make you stronger, more compassionate and will give you the ability and tools to overcome other seemingly negative struggles that may appear in your life. In short, your overcoming of RJ will make the world a better place. It is the best thing that I have ever done and I want you to thrive from the same results. You were not brought into this world to suffer. You are a divine, unique being that exists here for a positive reason.

So you have decided that the journey towards RJ's defeat **starts now**. Read on with a sense of courage, positivity, and lust for change!

Before we begin, just take these simple truths with you and review them regularly throughout your healing journey.

1. You will be gone one day. All of your possession will eventually turn to dust. Your loved ones will eventually be gone and so will any of your accomplishments, achievements, awards, and accolades. This is not written to depress you, quite the opposite. It is written to inspire you to grasp the reality of the finiteness of

all things. Life is simply too short for your RJ. You cannot allow it to remain as it is. Your life is there to be enjoyed and to share your uniqueness and love with the world.

2. Every moment of every one of your days on this earth is precious. Do not squander precious moments fighting with ungraspable, self-created demons.

3. You are a powerful, intelligent life force that is capable of manifesting almost anything into your world.

4. You are a unique human being. There is only one of you. You are the only being on the planet that has your unique fingerprints. You are a precious, powerful creation.

5. We are all connected. You have the same core fears, pains, emotions and needs as your fellow man/woman.

CHAPTER 1: MY STORY

I seemed to destroy every romantic relationship in which I had ever been involved. Not because of infidelity or incompatibility, not even because of fights, boredom, or need for personal space. They were all destroyed because of a trance-like state that would consume my entire being on an extremely regular basis. Almost as if I were possessed by a demonic entity. I would become hyper-vigilant, as observant as a private investigator. I would become a quick and intensely sharp manipulator. Warm anxiety imbrued energy would rapidly swell up from my feet to my stomach, all the way up my throat. I would lose control of my thoughts and words. All of these symptoms were seemingly caused by my obsession with my partner's past. I would bombard my partners with personal questions about their previous relationships. No stone would be left unturned and the obsessions would fester for days, weeks, months and years at a time. A myriad of imaginary images and thoughts of my partner's past would be cycling through my mind minute after minute with no respite. And when I finally went to sleep, I would suffer an onslaught of nightmares, watching these re-imagined past encounters of my partner play out like a movie. In waking I would name, blame, and call my partners all kinds of derogatory names. I wasn't consciously aware enough to control the outward assault on the world and the people around me. I lost wonderful people from my life as a result. I would feel sick as if I had some kind of virus in my bloodstream.

It wasn't until a serious relationship in my mid-twenties that I realized that this behavior was not the norm and it didn't meet my standards and values for what was ok and right. Up until this point, I could not imagine how anyone could **not** agree with me and be okay with their partner having any kind of intimate past with anyone else. After one particularly egregious RJ triggered fight with my partner, I watched her become so upset and broken down that it forced me to see clearly for the first time that my way of thinking was fueled by my jealousy and was not of sound thought. After this epiphany, I realized that I did not want to lose another close person in my life, and I knew deep down that it was time for change.

I first met Sarah four years before we had embarked on our relationship. Meeting at a gathering at a mutual friend's house, we quickly became friends. Because the friendship lasted many years before the relationship started, I was filled in on much of her intimate relationship based history and encounters. This information would be used as ammunition in my future jealousy fueled assaults. As the relationship progressed and we became a couple, I would question her more and more about her past, filling in mental timelines and imaginary puzzle pieces to create my own personalized images of what I thought happened, with snippets of slyly and not so slyly gathered information. At the beginning of the relationship, she would easily and innocently give in to my requests for information. My newly gathered information would trigger an emotionally insecure outburst from me and she would be left confused and distraught. She learned quickly and caught on to when I was trying to pull details from her past out of her and would close up, being very careful to not escalate my jealous state. Because of this, it caused emotional walls and barriers to go up at an early stage of the relationship. These walls blocked off much of our true potential connection. Not a day went by where I was not obsessing over one of her exes. I would attempt to snoop so far back into her history that even she could not remember the details of her past. I would place the imaginary puzzle pieces together for her and create my own film reels, ready to be played on loop in the Retroactive Jealousy movie theatre in my head. Anything she said would be mentally noted down and used against her. As our fights become more frequent, they would escalate, often to the point of near breakup. The thought of breaking up offered me an intense feeling of relief, as I would no longer have to think about her past and I could let her go. In truth, I was trying to let her past that I had conjured up in my head go, not her. I was not consciously aware enough at the time to realize that if I left the relationship, the relief would be very, very short-lived. I may be free of RJ for a certain length of time. But, as I embarked on a new relationship in the future and those familiar, exciting feelings would emerge all over again, so would my RJ triggers, despair and all of the nightmarish drama to accompany it. I thank the heavens that I was matched with someone so strong to her core that she would not leave me and vowed to work with me through it no matter how bad it got. Even when I proclaimed that I would never get better (it may feel like this when you are suffering with RJ). If your partner is not this supportive then have no fear. The problem does not lie with them, you must transform yourself from the inside, regardless of any external support system or loved one's involvement. The problem did not lie with Sarah, the problem was deep inside of me. I had to get to the core of my pain. Why was I so worried about these guys from her past? Why did I care so much about the details of these men to the point of unhealthy obsession? The journey for these answers led me to discover so much about myself, including who I really was and what I truly wanted in life. But first, I needed to not only subdue the pain so I could see clearly enough to grow, but I needed to go deep into the root of my pain and rip it out with both hands. Through time, much self-reflection and hard work, I was able to get better. I have since never been happier.

My journey towards healing began with the aforementioned epiphany that the way I was acting was not okay, nor was it conducive to any kind of enjoyable life for me or my partner. This led to an extensive online search wherein I tried to scrape together any information I could on any jealousy sufferers that had similar symptoms to me. This was when I made the groundbreaking discovery that this kind of jealousy had a name; Retroactive Jealousy. Up until this point, I had simply just named my behavior as plain old jealousy. As you likely have already discovered for yourself, RJ is not just boring old standard jealousy. To find out that I was not alone was massively comforting. I found some helpful resources and even discovered a facebook group of RJ sufferers! I did, however, encounter much counterproductive, insensitive information and "help" online which obviously was not produced by someone that had suffered with RJ. The kind of articles that offer such unhelpful nonsense as "their past doesn't matter, you just need to get over it, everybody's done something". As you have likely found, this kind of advice is fleetingly relieving at best, and probably trigger inducing quickly thereafter.

As I discovered more and more about RJ and the sufferers across the globe, I was overwhelmed with a new sense of fighting spirit and optimism that told me "this can be done! I can get through this!". Prior to this time, I had proclaimed the same old broken record statement of "I will never get better". As you speak, so shall you become. I began to turn this internal language around very quickly. Reversing my negative self-talk was a huge ally in my recovery. As I become more aware of my emotions and behaviors, I started questioning every aspect of my emotional states. Through much reading and study, I began to understand more about myself. One of the areas of my self that I became aware of was my intense fear and nervousness when out and about in public at night. I had always experienced these feelings but they were always under the surface and I was not consciously aware of them. As I dived deeper into why I felt this way, memories of violence inflicted upon me by older kids in my youth began to surface. I began seeing a therapist recommended by a family member. During my work with the therapist, I discovered that these feelings of fear and stress under the surface were affecting much of my life, not just when I was in public at night and felt vulnerable. I had unwittingly carried the emotional scars and fear inflicted on me as a child into my adult life. This discovery made me realize why I felt so weak and small in comparison to my partner's exes (who I had imagined and told myself were stronger, taller and overall more physically impressive then I was). It all started to come together piece by piece. My fear, my weakness, my sense of vulnerability. It all stemmed from my simple case of insecurity. Had I experienced scenarios in my youth where I had felt and appeared strong, courageous and heroic as opposed to weak and oppressed, I likely would have carried this into my adult subconscious mind and perhaps RJ would have never inhabited my being. It became clear that much of what I suffered from as an adult was a direct result of certain experiences in my youth. I had to correct these unhealthy subconscious habits that were tearing me down. I would later get in touch with my inner child.

(One book that helped me accomplish this inner child healing was 'Healing the Shame That Binds You' by John Bradshaw.)

I had discovered that many of my adult insecurities were stemmed from the fact that deep inside, I felt weak, small and vulnerable. This was a huge discovery as this meant that now I knew what I was working with. I could battle my issue with its polar opposite. If I felt weak, then I had to find a way to feel strong. If I felt shame then I had to combat this with confidence. If I felt fear then I had to combat this with courage.

I provide you with this information with the hope that you will search deep inside yourself to find out exactly what it is that makes you so insecure. It is likely stemming from your youth. I recommend you seek a therapist and have them aid you in getting to know your inner child. There are likely some life experiences that have caused you to become an adult that is not comfortable in their own skin; an adult with insecurities powerful enough to conjure up a beast such as Retroactive Jealousy. I eventually worked on my weakness issues by joining a Muay Thai class (and literally became a fighter), becoming a member of a gym and re-training my subconscious mind to replace the negative self-talk with affirmations of confidence and power.

With much research fresh in my mind, a wonderful therapist and a new understanding of myself, I had plenty of areas in which to begin my healing work. After about 18 months of dedicated, strategic and relentless transformative work, I was, in fact, free of RJ's insidious grip. Triggers would often continue to try and capture my attention but to no avail. I was too good at ignoring triggers. I was too good at focusing on the positive and my mind was occupied by wonderful, life-affirming thoughts and activities. Now, sometime later, I am 100% free of triggers, intrusive RJ thoughts and all of the destructive drama that accompanies them. You can be too! My relationship has also never been better. Read on with gusto!

✤ 2 ✤
CHAPTER 2: ACCEPTING RESPONSIBILITY AND COMING TO TERMS WITH YOUR ISSUES

At 25 years of age, it suddenly dawned on me that it was not normal for someone to act the way I was acting. I realized that the way I had been treating those closest to me was not acceptable, and for the first time, I truly accepted that I had a problem. My RJ based past perspective was one of not understanding how anyone else didn't join me in being absolutely distraught by their partner's past. My healed perspective is a full acceptance of what is and one of spreading full love and growth. It is often quite normal for a man or woman to be slightly upset or jealous upon hearing of their partner's previous relationships. But by contrast, for the RJ sufferer, jealousy can be joy denying and agonizing when it takes over and diminishes your way of life. Being in the grips of Retroactive Jealousy can feel like an absolute nightmare.

You must accept full responsibly for your RJ. It is not your partner's problem, it is yours. It is also not your partner's fault that you are afflicted. You must own it and accept it to become set up for real change. It is neither your fault that you are afflicted with RJ, but you must own it fully. You do not necessarily need to figure out the reason why you suffer from it. That is somewhat irrelevant (although finding out the root cause can often provide clarity and may aid in healing. I recommend this highly). If you were in the wilderness and shot with an arrow, you must first heal the wound and stop the poison before searching into the foliage for who shot the arrow. Later on, we will look at digging up the roots of your pain in Chapter 3: Facing Core Issues.

Without truly owning your Retroactive Jealousy, you may continue to blame your partner for their past and outwardly express your pain in a damaging way to those around you. Their past is not a problem. Their past is not here and now; the only time we will ever have. When suffering from RJ, it may feel like you are being cheated on by your partner at this very moment. This is because your body cannot differentiate between what is real and imaginary. It reacts chemically from the thoughts you present it with. Many anxiety sufferers feel like a lion is about to attack them, or a serial killer is going to invade their home. This is the body's defense mechanism to protect you. If one closes their eyes and imagines opening their fridge door, reaching in, picking out a lemon and taking a huge bite into it, one may find that their mouth begins to salivate. We know consciously that there is no lemon there, but the body's natural mechanism still does its job regardless of tangible objects, threats or surroundings. It is important to keep this in mind on your journey toward overcoming RJ.

Your partner's past does not exist. When you are battling with these thoughts, you are battling with a phantom. You cannot beat RJ by battling thoughts and you can't beat it by wrestling with a ghost, or an imaginary illusion. The first step to transforming your pain into power is to take ownership of your RJ. If you own it, you can transform this painful energy into life-affirming, loving power that will change your life forever. The strength you gain after transforming this RJ energy is courage inducing and will aid you through all of your life's endeavors.

Use a written/spoken affirmation technique to fully take ownership or you RJ.

Write the following affirmations down on paper and say them to yourself twice a day for the next week while you are starting your transformative journey. Say them once in the morning as you awake and once at night before you fall asleep.

1. I, take full ownership of my Retroactive Jealousy.
2. I, refuse to blame others for their past.
3. I, refuse to blame others for my suffering.

4. I, know that I and only I am responsible for my healing.
5. I, will not relent until I have transformed my RJ pain into powerful life-affirming energy.

Feel the power of taking ownership of your RJ. Once you own it, you can transform it.

CHAPTER 3: FACING CORE ISSUES HEAD-ON

You must find the positive opposite and remedy for every affliction you find shadowing over your life. For example; one of my core issues was that I felt physically and mentally weak. This insecurity gave my RJ plenty of mind food that would manifest as rapid-fire emotional triggers. This unbearable trigger ammo was based on believing that my partner had been involved with taller, more muscular and what I deemed as 'superior' men. Upon intense detective like interrogation from me, my partner would regularly pacify my OCD cycles by explaining that she was interested in me and not these taller, differently physiqued men (she was unknowingly enabling me and therefore thwarting my healing process). However, the trigger was already set, hidden under the leaves of my mind, waiting for the next upset. Then like clockwork, my mind would again be quickly caught in the seemingly inescapable bear trap.

Over time and with much work, a more conscious, positive side of my mind began to emerge whilst my RJ triggered thoughts lay struggling in the wilderness.

AFTER ONE PARTICULAR THERAPY SESSION, I WENT DEEP AND DISCOVERED the root cause of my feeling of weakness and inferiority. "Have you ever suffered any violence in your past?" asked my therapist. I thought way back to when I was twelve years old. I was out skateboarding with five or so of my friends and we had traveled through an underpass leading to a field surrounded by woodland on our way to the local skate park. A rowdy group of what seemed to be at least twenty to twenty-five older kids emerged from the trees, hurling profanities at us as we walked with our heads down, scared but minding our own business. The older group seemed to be in their late teens and early twenties. As the gang closed in, my friends in front of the group were attacked with punches to their heads and faces. As they ran ahead to get away, one friend was caught in the mayhem and had been beaten to the ground. I didn't want to run and leave my friend, so I hung back for him, I was also paralyzed with fear. I watched as several of the gang stamped his head against the concrete path (he escaped with no serious injuries). After they were done with him, they turned to me. I was surrounded by what seemed like 10 of them. One punched me hard across my face. So hard in fact, that my face went numb. The sensation was similar to the sensation of a football accidentally hitting your face on the playing field. It felt like my nose was where my ear should be. I heard from the right of me "This is how you do it!" And a swinging fist caught me deliberately in the throat. I fell to my knees and could not catch my breath. I was then punched more times then I could even feel around my face and head. As the beating continued, a passerby walking his dog was crossing the adjacent field and shouted to the gang "leave him alone!". "What are you gonna do about it?" Screamed the gang's ringleader. At that moment, I saw the only adult that could have rescued me turn away and leave the scene in fear. I felt truly helpless. One of the louts proceeded to pull a thick rope with a noose already tied out of a black hefty trash bag. I looked at the slipknot, then at the surrounding trees. My pupils dilated and I was filled with survival urges and adrenaline. It was fight or flight. With tremendous fear, I could sense what was about to happen. Before any savagery could continue, I saw an opening between the gang members' legs. With nothing to lose, I hopped through their legs and ran as fast as I could while leaving a bloody trail behind me. They followed and were close behind. My legs felt like jelly, but I kept running and running. I eventually saw a house, banged on the front door and an elderly couple, seeing the sense of panic on my face, let me in. They must have been utterly shocked. I managed to call the police and I was finally safe.

. . .

ALTHOUGH I GOT AWAY RELATIVELY UNHARMED PHYSICALLY, WHAT WAS left was a deep scar that would affect me for the rest of my life. I had unconsciously and unwittingly carried this egregious terror into my adult years. I firmly believe that this violent trauma was a strong fundamental cause of my retroactive jealousy as an adult. The lack of self-esteem and feeling of absolute helplessness and fear was one of the main blueprints for my eventual retroactive jealousy's towering architecture. The scared kid being beaten so fiercely was not ever truly dealt with and led to me remaining as that scared kid well into my adult life. I had discovered the potential root of not only my low self-esteem issues but also my internalized shame. I had a hard time being in public without looking over my shoulder and any aggression from anyone else in any other scenario throughout my life would trigger a similar fear that I felt that day when I was twelve years old. The inferiority complex seed had been sown in the soil of fear and it was only a matter of time before the sprouts of retroactive jealousy would appear.

I TELL YOU THIS STORY BECAUSE THE REDISCOVERY OF THIS TRAUMA HELPED me get deep enough inside of my head to figure out why I felt so weak and why I had such an issue with my partner's ex's whom I deemed so superior to myself. Finding this trauma again was enough of an epiphany for me to realize that my feelings of weakness and low self-esteem were not pulled out of thin air and I wasn't born with them. They were learned, and as with most mental patterns, can be unlearnt! I went to the root of the problem; why I felt inferior. I ripped out the roots that lay deep in the under layers of my consciousness by learning to become strong. A powerful tool in my healing path was utilizing a wonderful therapist that I felt comfortable confiding in. Finding a fantastic therapist can be an unbelievable help, not only in the healing of your RJ but in many areas of your life. Although it is not imperative that you discover why you suffer from RJ (some sufferers may seem to have no reason at all), it may benefit you to find root causes and remove them. It helped me on my path but you **can** beat it without truly knowing why you're afflicted. Ask yourself; why do you suffer from RJ? I urge you to look far into your past, into your youth. You may just find the answer.

. . .

So how did I combat this inferiority complex that made me feel so weak? I became a fighter, in the most literal sense of the word. I felt weak, so I decided to become the polar opposite. I decided to become strong. Please pay attention to the word **decided!** I started training and studying Muay Thai in a mixed martial arts gym. I felt so shy and weak when I first walked into the gym. The sound of punch bags being aggressively kicked echoed throughout the huge warehouse, and the sounds of budding fighters being slammed to the matt in the Brazilian Jiu-Jitsu cage hit my eardrums with an excitement inducing thud. I had found a place where my shyness, strength, and fortitude would be tested. After my first training session, I felt a sense of control, power, and courage. The shy, weak boy was transforming into something completely new. I fell in love with the art of eight limbs and had found an activity that made me feel on top of the world. This time when I was being punched in the head or kicked in the face (pads included)! I welcomed it. I could feel my strength growing with every strike received and every strike launched from my limbs. I quickly found myself sparring with the kinds of men I had felt so inferior to before, and I was holding my own! This gifted me a whole new level of healthy confidence that I had not experienced before. The weak kid was not weak anymore. This new physical strength paved the way for mental strength. This newly found confidence was one of the main weapons in my arsenal in the battle against RJ. Over the next several months of training, I would pay close attention to how my RJ would react in an environment where I would be given the tools to summon inner and outer strength. A place where I could transform my body and mind to become a more powerful version of myself. RJ could not exist here in the gym. It was being starved off from any negative mind food. I was too active and working too hard for RJ to get my attention. RJ would often strike after I had arrived home from training, but this time it was facing a far tougher opponent than it was previously used to. An opponent who's healthy self-esteem was growing rapidly. RJ's time was running out and it was becoming clear that it could not withstand many more rounds in the ring. I kept training for a while until my RJ had shrunk to the point of no return. I viewed my Muay Thai training sessions more like mental therapy sessions as opposed to just physical workouts. This helped me conjure the motivation to travel to the Muay Thai gym and train weekly, as the sessions were helping me mentally in ways I had not experienced before. With the diminishment of my RJ, I slowly stopped training periodically as other areas and goals in my life became more of a priority to me. But although I didn't continue to train as vigilantly as I once did, one thing remains; my Muay Thai training was one of the greatest and beneficial endeavors I ever embarked on. I will now live the rest of my life with more confidence, strength and personal power that I previously could have thought possible. Not to mention, it gives me great inner courage knowing that I can protect my family more than I ever could before. These positive feelings and emotions are all potent RJ repellent. Remember the beginning of this book when I told you RJ was one of the best things to ever happen to me? Well, I would not have developed these positive mindsets, physical skills and emotions had I not gone through it.

OBVIOUSLY BECOMING A FIGHTER IS NOT FOR EVERYONE. BUT THE MESSAGE here is that you need to find **your** Muay Thai. Whether it is yoga, weight training, making more money, painting, cycling or even cooking. It doesn't matter what it is. The fact is that there is something out in the world you can do that will combat your negative thoughts about your self and raise your self-esteem. I realized after some training that I was far stronger than I ever thought I could be. Find whatever it is that will boost your self-esteem and go for it relentlessly! This will be a major tool in your healing process. Don't wait! ACT NOW! Start today!

❦ 4 ❦
CHAPTER 4: DEALING WITH TRIGGERS

I f you are reading this book and are suffering with Retroactive Jealousy, then you are most likely extremely familiar with triggers. They are the ever-waiting and patient RJ's favorite tool to use against you when it is ready to feed again. If you have ever suffered from obsessive-compulsive disorder, or are familiar with the symptoms, then you will likely notice a resemblance between OCD intrusive thoughts and RJ's use of triggers. They are much the same in characteristics. Many Retroactive Jealousy resources state RJ as a type of obsessive-compulsive disorder. As I am not trained in the area of psychology or cognitive behaviors, I am not qualified to diagnose or compare symptoms. I will, however, mention that I have suffered from many OCD traits throughout my life and thought it somewhat of a coincidence that I also suffered from RJ so severely. I would regularly find myself acting out several OCD patterns such as constant checking of door locks and intrusive thoughts (not just relating to my partner's past). You may want to look further into OCD, it's traits and likeness to RJ's intrusive thoughts and triggers, as there may be some other areas of your life that OCD may have a foothold. Although, as I mention elsewhere in this book, it is not imperative that you understand the actual cause of your RJ. It is, however, imperative to a healthy life and future that you transform these painful experiences into personal power.

Triggers will appear of their own accord and will strike as if they had a life of their own. They may appear first thing in the morning and they may appear as you lay down to sleep. They may appear when you pass a bar or restaurant that your partner used to frequent with an ex, or you may hear a song on the radio from a band your partner went to see live with an ex. All triggers can be equally as painful and are ingenious and cunning in enchanting you into a trance-like panic state. You cannot control when these triggers strike, but, with practice, you can control your reaction to them!

You cannot overcome or beat your triggers, but, you can starve them. They feed on your emotional reactions and thoughts. One exercise that helped me was picturing my triggered thoughts waves in a blue ocean. The thought is just a wave that will pass. All thoughts are fleeting and will pass relatively quickly when they are not powered by emotional reactions. Simply watch the wave rise and fall without getting emotionally involved with it. When you feel the emotion rise in your stomach, just let it be, breathe deeply and don't feed the thought. The mind is quick and will rapidly move on to something else. The previous negative trigger thought will be discarded until it strikes again, this time weaker, and eventually not at all. When you are not thinking about it, it does not exist. With practice, this method will starve your bombarding thoughts from negative emotional interaction, thus killing off RJ's most powerful weapon; triggers.

DON'T TALK ABOUT IT!

Refrain from talking about your triggers! You may feel the urge to discuss the jealousy infused thoughts and even question your partner about them. Don't give in! The more you talk about your RJ thoughts, the more food you feed them, and the more power you give them, lengthening their lifespan. The faster you learn to stop talking about your triggers, the faster you will overcome Retroactive Jealousy. This is by far one of the most difficult tasks to master, but extremely crucial to your recovery. Try to find some kind of engaging thought form to overtake your attention. Whenever I felt the urge to bombard my partner with questions, I would practice challenging piano scales in my mind, with my hands executing the movements in the air.

KEEP A TRIGGER DIARY

Another method that helped me heal was keeping a trigger diary. I kept a notebook with me at all times. Whenever I was triggered I would write down the time and date and what the trigger inducing thought was. At first, this was a method of tracking my recovery progress. As the days and weeks went by, I would revisit my trigger diary and review the previous entries. I would be analytical of my triggers and notice that the entries were often very similar in content but sometimes focused on slightly different aspects of my partner's past. I may have been ruminating over a particular one of my partner's ex's in one week and another the next. Slowly, upon review of these entries, I started to notice that they didn't necessarily have the power to ruin my day. I survived the days in which I was previously triggered and I lived to fight another day. They were not the end of the world. I would think to myself "Oh here's that thought about that one guy again, just like yesterday, and the day before that!". I pondered the almost comical idea that I could set my watch to the times I was triggered by a particular thought. By entering my triggers into this diary, I was exposing RJ's bag of tricks and bringing them into the light of my awareness. Once you become consciously aware of RJ's tricks, they start to lose their power over you little by little. One day as I was scanning over my past entries, I came to the realization; I did not feel the same amount of grief from the triggers that I had entered previously in weeks gone by. My triggers were shrinking in power, and I was on my way to recovery.

MEDITATION AND SPIRITUALITY

Meditation is an extremely powerful tool that will aid you on your healing path. Meditation was one of the most valuable tools in transforming my Retroactive Jealousy and is one of the most life-altering resources you can use at any moment. At the time of writing this book, I have meditated almost every day for the past 3 years and will continue to do so for the rest of my life. The benefits are endless and I have never been so happy or been able to access such tranquil states of peace in my life. We spend so much of our time being lost and trying to grab hold of the past and we spend so much time worrying about the future, that we are rarely ever here and now; the only thing we will ever have. The past does not exist, the future is simply a thought. To access the present moment is to be free of the imaginary chains of your past and future. Meditation is a way of accessing the present moment with your focus. When you are present in the now, RJ cannot inhabit you, as it is simply brought about by a myriad of thought-forms. When you meditate and are present in the now, you transcend all thought and cut off RJ's food supply. It cannot live in the present moment if you become fully present. "Well, how do I access this presence? How do I meditate?" I hear you asking. I have outlined my daily meditation practice below.

1. Find a quiet area where you will not be disturbed.
2. Set an alarm for ten minutes from now.
3. Sit on the floor and cross your legs, place your hands on your knees with your palms facing upward in receiving mode.
4. Close your eyes and take in a deep breath for five seconds, hold for five seconds, release the breath for five seconds. Repeat.
5. Focus on your breath and listen to the silence that pervades the room. Try to not get attached to any thoughts that might appear and let them dissolve peacefully in the silence.
6. Feel the inner body by focusing on the energy pulse that you can feel naturally in your hands.
7. The mind will often creep in and try to take over. This is normal and natural. Don't scold yourself for losing focus, just gently bring your focus back to your breath and the silence.

Repeating this simple meditation daily will help you to cultivate presence and will develop your ability to tap into this peaceful silence. A space of no thought. Another benefit of meditation is the separation from your being and your mind made ego. I do not use the term ego in a derogatory way to describe an egomaniac or traits of narcissism. I use the word ego to describe that personality, character or individual which you think you are. Essentially, everything you think you are; your name, job title, political views, passions, and values were all made up at some point. They do not exist on any plain other than being thought-forms. Any physical or tangible evidence that would argue the contrary was simply manifested out of the made-up thought-forms. You may have many certificates saying that you are adept at a certain skill or have flourished in a certain career path, but none of these past accolades, trophies or endeavors are in fact who you really are. This is not to say that there are not wonderful careers and lives to be led, this is just to bring to your attention to the fact that nothing is absolutely true. This is why we are able to reprogram our subconscious minds with new thought-forms about ourselves. Everything is or was just made up at one time or another.

Starting a meditation practice and reading spiritual books gave me a whole new sense of being. I recommend it for everyone, especially if one is suffering from an affliction such as Retroactive Jealousy. Set aside 10 minutes daily to meditate starting today! I usually meditate first thing in the morning. I wake up, smile, rehydrate and immediately sit down to meditate. This has become the beginning of my daily morning ritual. With practice, you can enter a whole new state of being. One where RJ cannot inhabit.

Two books I highly recommend in the topic of spirituality and meditation are Eckhart Tolle's 'The Power of Now' *and* Eckhart Tolle's 'A New Earth'

CHAPTER 5: POSITIVE ACTION AND POSITIVE ADDICTIONS

The Myriad of harmful and potentially life diminishing addiction based scenarios we can find ourselves in is endless. Devastating addictions to drugs, alcohol, nicotine, and gambling run rampant in our world and have destroyed countless lives. We have all seen the screaming vagrant in the street or the drunk in the gutter.

But what about the positive addictions that we can invite into our lives? What about the go-getters and the winners? What about the athlete who is at the top of their game, the world-class musician or the entrepreneur whose businesses are skyrocketing? What do they have that the majority does not? I believe that their success is mostly due to an insatiable addiction to progress, gains and achieving goals.

As a kid, I would become obsessed with leveling up my character in my favorite video game. With each battle, he would become stronger and stronger, and with each victory, he would gain experience. I became addicted to my character's growth until eventually I had completed the game and destroyed the evil villain that was threatening my fictional protagonist's world! I was a relatively lazy kid outside of video games. I would sleep in late, put off homework and would study the bare minimum I needed to get by. As I grew up and became involved in different activities such as playing the piano, martial arts training, and art, I noticed that my video game positive growth addiction had actually carried over into my real-world activities. I was improving at my hobbies and endeavors because I felt the same buzz I felt when I leveled up my video game character. I realized this 'buzz' wasn't exclusive to just video games and hobbies. As an adult, the same buzz would also kick in once I had powered through a great work out at the gym, hit a financial goal, or studied a new book and expanded my knowledge. Somewhere along the line, I had become addicted to growth and progress. It may have happened naturally. It may have been passed down from hard-working parents. But it is my strong belief that no matter what your background or situation, you can train your brain to develop these positive addictions in the same way that you may have developed a buzz training up your favorite video game character as a kid or mastering a new skateboard trick.

When you achieve, celebrate your achievement! Acknowledge it and own it. If you find that you dealt with an RJ trigger without becoming emotionally attached to it, then celebrate it. If you saw your partners ex in the street and dealt with the trigger better than you would have before, then celebrate your growth. Start associating good feelings with your achievements, you have earned it. I don't mean crack open a beer and get wild (alcohol often negatively affects RJ drastically and can inhibit your ability to cope with triggers). A little buzz of happiness is enough to push you through and continue the cycle of positive growth. Happiness breeds more happiness, and happiness is power. It is life-affirming. Happiness is a powerful tool to utilize for your healing. RJ cannot swim for long in the rushing waves of true happiness associated with progress and enjoyment of your craft, career or hobbies. Your positive addition when teamed up with your new methods of dealing with triggers will form a dynamic state altering duo to aid you on your journey towards a life without RJ.

AFFIRMATIONS

Affirmations are a brilliant way to boost whatever particular state you are trying to improve. I often interchange my affirmations by which state I want to get into at that particular time of my life. For example; if I want to build confidence then I will recite ten or more confidence-boosting affirmations a day. If I am in a phase in my life where I want to overcome shyness and become better at interacting with people then I will recite ten or more affirmations that may instill bravery and courage within me. Keep repeating these affirmations day after day, week after week and month after month and see what happens. The affirmations will soak into your subconscious mind and you will train your brain to believe. This is a powerful method also used to manifest material or financial abundance. As mentioned in the previous chapter, everything is made up. So make up your own story, your own new and improved version of yourself free of RJ. You can even sleep with affirmations being played to you via recording. I often find affirmation videos I like on YouTube and will fall asleep to them. I recommend creating ten or more affirmations yourself that will boost your positive outlook on your healing process. I have created ten below for you. If you feel silly saying them out loud then just say them in your mind or quietly to yourself. If you don't truly believe the affirmations then fake it until you make it. This may sound like self-help mumbo jumbo to some readers, but if you're serious about moving on from your RJ then try it and see for yourself! Programming the subconscious mind can change your life.

POSITIVE GROWTH AFFIRMATIONS

1. I am powerful.
    2. I am enough.
    3. I am worthy.
    4. I am confident.
    5. I am strong.
    6. I am attractive
    7. I am desirable.
    8. I feel inferior to no one.
    9. Others look up to me.
    10. Others respect me.

❦ 6 ❦
CHAPTER 6: CHANGING HOW YOU FEEL ABOUT YOURSELF

How do you feel about yourself? Is your day filled with negative self-talk? Do you regularly internally mutter things like "I hate myself, I'm a loser, I can't compare to him/her" and so on. I would have a stream of this negative self-talk going on all day, every day until I became consciously aware of it. This internal negative self-talk is like a poisonous waterfall relentlessly flowing through your lifestream. You must become aware of this internal dialogue and replace these savage words with their positive opposites. "I hate myself" becomes "I love myself". "I am a loser" becomes "I am a winner". No matter how silly, arrogant or conceited this positive self-talk sounds, it is imperative to your internal uprising of happiness. Try it for yourself with an open mind and reap the benefits. Much like how a vibration of gratefulness will bring about more positive situations in your life, this internal attitude of confidence will bring about self-power and manifest positivity. The negative outburst of others will begin to roll off your back with enough self-work. You will become so comfortable in your own skin that your RJ and triggers will find this confident habitat toxic and unbearable. Your RJ will have no negative food to eat and grow from. After all, your RJ likely stems and thrives from your insecurity and not being comfortable or confident in your own skin.

Imagine your own personal greatest version of yourself. What do they look like? What is their primary attitude? How do they react to certain situations? Are they confident and assertive? Are they strong and centered? Are they outgoing and successful? Are they plagued with jealousy and strive to control others, or are they relaxed, calm and need no external enablers?

Spend a few minutes closing your eyes and brainstorming your ideal version of yourself. Be as outlandish as your imagination lets you. Hold nothing back. This ideal you should have all of the attributes you aspire to have in your life. Once you have a solid image in your mind of this ideal you, you must commit to taking daily steps to become this version of yourself. Life is simply too short **not** to become this you. Write down on paper at least 10 character/physical traits that your ideal version of you possesses.

Is your ideal you in incredible shape? This is attainable for you. Is your ideal you oozing with confidence and coolness? This too is attainable for you. Does your ideal you acquire a substantially larger income than you possess right now? There has been no better time in history to build online businesses and find alternative sources of income, both passive and active. Does your ideal you possess incredible knowledge that can be used to enrich your life? We live in the digital age where you can find online courses on just about anything you can think of that will ultimately enhance and enrich your life, all available at the click of a button. You can attain any outcome you desire for yourself. We may be partially limited to changing our outer appearance (although plastic surgeons are remarkable these days!), but the inner work we can do is unbelievably transformative when practiced with gusto and enthusiasm. I was once a shy, scared adult child. I am now a confident, assertive and successful man. This was done by first imagining my ideal self, then taking a stand to become that version of myself and not wavering my gaze from the destination; a new and improved me.

Some attributes that I wished to possess (pre RJ recovery) were as follows:

Attribute 1: Confident, assertive and comfortable in own skin.
How I achieved this attribute in reality:
• Programming my subconscious mind by using confidence affirmations (usually on drives to the gym and in headphones as I went to sleep at night).
• Getting my body into shape by daily gym workouts.
• Learning Muay Thai and developing self-defense skills and discipline.

Attribute 2: Unaffected by RJ. Unphased by intrusive thoughts and triggers.
How I achieved this attribute in reality:
Daily meditation work. Practice living in the now.
Breathing/meditation work to let go of triggered thoughts as they arise.
Practiced allowing intrusive thoughts to be without trying to stop them or
getting emotionally attached to them.

Attribute 3: A sense of strength and being able to defend myself. No longer
feeling physically weak and vulnerable.
How I achieved this attribute in reality:
Getting my body into shape by daily gym workouts.
Learning Muay Thai and developing self-defense skills and discipline.
Sparring in Muay Thai classes (holding my own against men that were
physically larger than me did wonders for my self-esteem).
Achieving higher ranks in Muay Thai over time.

Attribute 4: Positive mood, happiness, general state of upbeat wellbeing.
How I achieved this attribute in reality:
Daily grateful statements as part of my morning ritual (see chapter 7).
Changing my diet. Daily juicing and smoothies to enhance my mood from
the inside.
Daily gym schedule.
Daily reading of spiritual and self-help books.

Attribute 5: Financially better off. Not detrimentally comparing oneself
financially to others.
How I achieved this attribute in reality:
• Started my own online business.
• Created new passive income streams. Increased income through a more
rigorous work ethic.
• Started investing.
• Studied many investing and business courses/books.

Attribute 6: A higher level of intellect and knowledge.
How I achieved this attribute in reality:
Studied many online courses and books. Many to do with finances, investing

and business.
Daily reading as part of my morning ritual.

Attribute 7: Enhanced physical appearance.
How I achieved this attribute in reality:
Change of diet.
Implementing a weekly gym schedule.
Staying hydrated.
Implementing daily skincare routine and bi-weekly derma roller schedule.
Changing the products I put on my face.
Keeping up with hair appointments and not appearing unkempt.
Routine grooming maintenance.
Keeping up with dental appointments and teeth cleanings.

Attribute 8: A strong work ethic. No laziness or procrastination.
How I achieved this attribute in reality:
Listening daily to self-help teachers podcasts and audiobooks.
Increased work ethic through determination to change.
Daily goal setting on whiteboard (crossing out goals from your whiteboard is addicting and sparks gusto!).
Setting alarms and reprogramming body clock to awake at an earlier time.
Implementing a morning ritual.
Cutting down television time and replacing this with studying, working or productive activities.

Attribute 9: Likable, conversational and a pleasure to be around.
How I achieved this attribute in reality:
Clearing the mind of unnecessary thoughts and emotional baggage through daily meditation practice and trigger work.
Staying grounded in presence.
Ceased seeing other human beings as separate entities or a threat by reading books on spirituality.
Meeting other human beings without making any initial judgment or assumptions of their character.
Smiling peacefully even in uncomfortable or undesirable situations.
Listening more often than speaking.

Attribute 10: More giving, loving and eager to share with the world.
How I achieved this attribute in reality:
Sharing useful knowledge with others that I have gained through life experiences and studying certain subjects.
Making my knowledge easily available to others at no cost to them.
Giving a percentage of my newly acquired income to a needy cause.
Helping others without expecting anything in return.

Attribute 11. Patience and kindness even when being confronted with argumentative conflict or difficult people.
How I achieved this attribute in reality:
• Daily meditation practice with a strong focus on my anger issues.
• Studying several self-help books that touch on psychology, gaining a deeper understanding of the human condition.
• Getting in touch with my empathetic side.
• Using patience and presence practices during personal relationship conflicts or situations. Working on fear of confrontation.

You may notice that I have mentioned some of the same activities aimed at improving yourself time and time again, such as working out at the gym, studying books/courses and implementing a morning ritual. This is because they work! Repetition is imperative to your success. Don't just work out once and then let your gym bag collect dust. Don't just read the first chapter of a new self-help book and stick it up on the shelf to never be picked up again. Make a habit of these attribute developing actions and they will truly become life-changing.

"I fear not the man who has practiced 10,000 kicks once, but I fear the man who has practiced one kick 10,000 times". Bruce Lee

Write down your own attributes that you would like to possess and start working toward them today! Your ideal version of yourself can be a reality. An RJ free you can be a reality.

Once you have recovered from your RJ you can take this new work ethic with you for every endeavor for the rest of your life! Beating RJ is one of the toughest things you will have to go through. But the transformative might its recovery yields is full great power. You can achieve anything with this newfound life-affirming power, drive and work ethic. You are in control. Make your life the way you want it by first changing yourself from the inside.

STOP COMPARING YOURSELF TO OTHERS

During my pre RJ recovery years, I would regularly find myself comparing my height, body, finances, personality, looks and just about everything else you can imagine to my partner's ex-lovers. This was an absolute waste of time. Even if I temporarily felt superior in one aspect, there would be another opposing attribute my mind would conjure up to quickly tear me down and make me obsess over this particular ex. Comparing yourself to others in a mental superiority test is a futile, agonizing and time-wasting endeavor. You will never find peace from this and it will only give your mind more food for your RJ to feast on and grow. One of the only times it will be beneficial to compare yourself to others is when you are learning and growing from them.

I would scroll through my partner's social media posts from years past to catch glimpses of her exes. I would try to see if I could compare my height or looks to them. While scrolling through these posts I would be in a trance-like state full of panic with my hands shaking and my mind super vigilant. I felt as if I were infected with some kind of virus. All these activities did was produce food for my RJ. How do you starve RJ to death? You stop serving it mind food that will sustain it. Comparing yourself to your partner's exes serves up one of RJ's favorite meals. It can feed off of this mind food for years, tormenting you day in and day out.

If you feel compelled to compare yourself to your partner's exes then try vigilantly to stop immediately in your tracks, breathe deeply, become present and remember your commitment to change. Remember the sweet benefits of change. I would often have to snap myself out of it quickly before embarking on a night of social media scrolling and the ensuing inevitable interrogation that I would dump onto my partner. They do not deserve it and it is your responsibility to change.

You are the only you in existence. You are a unique, beautiful, intelligent creation and you are worthy. You are not less than desirable. You are a magnificent creation of the universe.

❧ 7 ❧
CHAPTER 7: HAPPINESS IS POWER

When you are truly happy, filled with ecstatic energy and so excited that you feel like you want to run up a wall, you are in possession of powerful life affirming energy. This happiness energy is the creative source behind much art, music, literature and just about any other outlet of passion you can think of. It will also be an important force that will aid in your recovery from RJ. You may have read the first sentence of this chapter and thought,"filled with ecstatic energy and so excited that you feel like I want to run up a wall? Who does this author think he is? I never feel like this". This is because your mind has been overwhelmed with images of your partners past and has been tormenting you relentlessly, draining you of precious life energy. In these states of torment, it is most difficult to conjure up our happiness and implement a state of healing. But it is not impossible. Think back to before you suffered from Retroactive Jealousy, perhaps when you were a child. You were not bombarded with these painful RJ thoughts. Your mind had plenty of room to focus on all of the wonderful toys, games and activities you could enjoy. When you were triggered to be momentarily sad or unhappy, it was likely because of an immediate situation bought to your direct attention such as not getting the cookie or being told to do you chores. (This is assuming you had an upbringing in a non toxic environment household. If you were bought up in a toxic environment household then there will likely be much additional work to be done with a therapist. I highly recommend seeking a wonderful therapist that will fast track your road to recovery). As adults, our minds become overactive, usually due to our daily responsibilities such as paying the bills, feeding the kids and so on. Without the necessary work on ourselves to practice clearing our mind and accessing more peaceful states of consciousness, we often get caught up in the mental rat race of relentless, anxiety ridden thoughts. We take this to be the norm in our society and most of us go through our entire lives like this. When you were a child you likely focused on one thing at a time; what was immediately in front of you. You can practice this as an adult. It is an almost meditative like exercise that helps you access the present moment and focuses you fully on the task at hand. Try it now. Take several deep breaths down into your stomach. Now focus fully on this page for 10 seconds. Other thoughts may try to distract you and come in and out, but just hold your focus and gaze on the page. As you get better at this, then try 30 seconds, then one minute and so on. You will likely find that the quality of your work benefits greatly from this practice as your mind will not be elsewhere. You have re-learnt your childhood gift of present moment focus. Now try this focus on something fun. There is a reason many adrenaline junkies and daredevils love extreme sports, racing and sky diving. It takes their complete focus for a period of time.

FOCUS ON HAPPINESS CONJURING GOALS

If you take your focus from these intrusive RJ thoughts and replace them with happiness inducing tasks, thoughts or activities then it will fill you with the excitement, courage and life affirming power needed to recover from RJ. For me these thoughts included brainstorming my goals for the year. These may be financial, artistic or work related goals that excite me. This book you're reading right now was one of my goals. For example: this book excited me during its creation because I knew that I could help countless people suffering from RJ all around the world get better and transform their lives. What are some goals that excite you that you would like to accomplish? Write these down and keep them close to review regularly. I like to write mine out of a large whiteboard in my office. I get a huge buzz and sense of excitement when I cross an accomplished goals off of my list.

HAPPINESS THROUGH GRATEFULNESS

One transformative tool that aided me in my recovery was developing a huge feeling of gratitude. I practice this daily without fail (usually on the way to and from the gym). I always notice a huge wave of happiness overcome me during this part of my day. I include this gratefulness practice in my morning ritual. This practice involves saying out loud how grateful I am for certain things in my life. They can vary day by day and can range from silly little things such as; "I am so grateful that the weather is great today" to more important events such as; "I am so grateful and happy that my parents are in good health and I am able to call them whenever I can". Once you start saying these grateful phrases out loud you will start vibrating on a frequency of thankfulness. You may notice that you start to attract more good things into your life. I highly recommend you try this for yourself wether you believe in the power of manifestation and the law of attraction or not. Try it with an open mind, then make your verdict. My experience was that I started attracting wonderful things into my life. My family was happy, my finances were growing and my career started to take off wonderfully, just by saying how grateful I was for what I had every day. If finances are a stress trigger for you (or an RJ trigger by comparing yourself with your partners exes) then try to remember that most of the worlds population lives off of about two dollars per day. If you are reading this book on a phone, computer or iPad, then that makes you abundant and affluent in comparison to most of the worlds population! If you show gratitude for this fact regularly, then you will start to attract more of the same into your life.

I once had a friend who was convinced he was cursed. He would go on every day about how no one loved him, how he attracted bad luck and how he was a loser. As you can guess, his behavior manifested the equivalent outcomes of such a mindset. He was even physically beaten up two times just a few weeks apart of each other which is a horrible ordeal to go through, but it seemed as though the universe was listening to his requests. It was as if he was saying to the universe "beat me up, I'm trash". My friend soon lost his career, his friends, his home, his girlfriend and just about everything good that he had. His health was also deteriorating as he fed himself a diet of cigarettes and alcohol, and would only eat bread with ketchup day after day. He could have turned his life around and thrived had he changed his frequency to one of gratefulness and happiness. In reality he was talented, attractive, funny, kind and great to hang out with when he was not in his usual negative slump. He could have easily had anything he wanted in life, but it's not too late for him. Let's hope he learns the lessons that are in this book elsewhere and lives his life to the fullest without wasting another day. I often think of the tale of Aladdin and his magical lamp. Aladdin rubs the lamp and the genie appears. "Your wish is my command" says the genie. This is much like the universe listening to your wishes and requests. The universe is not biased and it listens to everything you send out to it. Why not try saying how thankful you are everyday for being free of Retroactive Jealousy? Even if you are not fully recovered yet, start acting as if you were and you will start to heal from the inside.

(One book that I thoroughly recommend if you have not already heard of it is 'The Secret' by Rhonda Byrne.)

Some examples of grateful statements I might say out loud each morning are:

"I am so grateful for my health".
"I am so grateful that my son is happy and healthy, and I have a wonderful relationship with him".
"I am so grateful for my career".
"I am so grateful for my work ethic".
"I am so grateful that I put healthy food into my body each day"
"I am so grateful for my wonderful relationship".
"I am so grateful for my talents".
"I am so grateful that I live in one of the most incredible places I could ever want to live".
"I am so grateful that I have great eyesight".
"I am so grateful for all of the hardships I have gone through, because they have made me strong and given me new found intelligence, power and tools".

These are just some examples, but have fun making up your own grateful statements. Get creative and say these aloud with a smile on your face. You can watch your world transform before your eyes!

HAPPINESS THROUGH ACTIVITIES

As I get lost in the enjoyment of activities, I notice that my mind is not focused on negative painful thoughts. This is a particularly helpful tool during your transformation of RJ. To be happy during an activity you love is a way to fill yourself with life affirming happiness power. The power will positively fuel your healing journey. This is not a method for merely periodically covering up your RJ. The goal is not to stick a band aid on the wound to cover it up for a while, nor distract us from the deep rooted issue. It is simply to bring more happiness and power into our life-force so that we can tackle RJ with our batteries recharged by a zest for life. Some activities I find give me happiness-strength are practicing the piano, Muay Thai, working out, reading/learning, and creating art. Notice how the activities I have mentioned help me grow either in terms of achieving new levels at an instrument, increasing my physical fitness or expanding my knowledge through reading. Growth through activities is not essential but you may find it gives you added gusto as the feeling of progress and growth often fills us with excitement. After a session of getting lost in these growth based activities, I find myself with a fresh mind and a sense of achievement that gives me additional strength and power to take on other tasks; such as defeating RJ! I am under the absolute conviction that happiness is true power. A way to be joyful is to dance amidst the external forms the universe provides and to emit the life affirming power into other forms. One activity that was personally essential to my overcoming RJ was a regular gym routine. The daily boost of endorphins was a chemical supplementary boost that often helped me access more peaceful states. This helped greatly in dealing with triggers and negative mind patterns.

❦ 8 ❧
CHAPTER 8: FINDING GREAT TEACHERS

One thing I am grateful for every day is the fact that we have access to countless teachers at the click of a button. Just by picking up our smartphones we can access countless hours of free knowledge from spiritual teachers, therapists, self-help coaches and more. There is no excuse not to learn and grow in this day and age. Long gone are the days of dragging yourself to the library to borrow a book for a week or two. Although that option also still exists. I often listen to spiritual teachers' guidance, entrepreneurs podcasts, and YouTubers' helpful knowledge whilst driving in my car and working out at the gym. Although I like to enjoy music daily, I always make sure I have a steady stream of new, useful, positive information being made available to my mind and subconscious programming.

Some spiritual teachers I enjoy are Eckhart Tolle, Adyashanti, Mooji, and Sadhguru. Their teachings have helped me reach a new state of consciousness where my old negative habits find it impossible to reside. Finding a spiritual teacher you like and adding their knowledge to a daily meditation practice is a surefire way to boost your RJ recovery and give you access to a higher state of consciousness that you can primarily reside in for the rest of your life. Once you have healed your RJ, you will be able to take your transformative tools with you anywhere you go in life. It won't just be your RJ that's transformed. You can transform huge areas of your life should you choose to. You likely will once you have the gusto of transforming your RJ pain into positive life energy.

One book that transformed my life is 'The Power of Now' by Eckhart Tolle. Eckhart's teaching states that the past nor the future exist, only now exists. The amount of truth exuded from the pages of Eckhart's book was enough to change my life forever and prevent me from going back to the way I had previously viewed the world. This was a transformative way of living that eventually withered away the power the past had over me. I had spent so much of my life living in the past and so much time worrying about the future that I had neglected that all I ever had and would ever have is right now in this very moment. A simple yet profound realization. Although not directly related to jealously or relationships, Eckhart Tolle's 'The Power of Now' remains a powerful companion by my side whenever life challenges me emotionally or mentally. This book was a must-read along my journey of RJ's transformation.

FINDING A GOOD THERAPIST

A powerful way to find out more about yourself and really dig to the root of your problems is to work with a therapist. It is important to find a therapist you like and enjoy your sessions with. It might take you a couple of tries to find one that you are fully comfortable with. If you like the first therapist you find then just go with it. Commit to a weekly session for a certain time period. You will likely be very glad you did. Weekly therapy sessions helped me understand certain childhood issues I was still carrying around with me as an adult. It helped me become self-aware of my many previously unconscious patterns and self-sabotage. Your RJ is likely a manifestation of unresolved childhood issues. For example; my RJ likely stemmed from a deep sense of shame I had unconsciously implemented as the default setting to how I saw myself in my youth. I also had unresolved trauma as a result of random violence inflicted on me many years ago. This was all unconscious and hiding under the surface, manifesting as negative, painful energy pulls, sabotaging my adult life. Going deep into my subconscious and remembering this violent incident helped me understand why I never felt safe out in public at night, even all these years later. It also made me realize why I felt so weak and small as an adult. I would likely have never bought these unresolved issues to the surface had I not committed to weekly therapy sessions with a wonderful therapist for a certain period of time. Once you discover these hidden issues, you must pull them out at the root. Your therapist will show you useful practices for weed pulling unresolved issues. Combine this approach with a daily meditation practice and an awakened spiritual teacher to create yourself a triple threat team ready to dissolve RJ and bring about a happier, more powerful you.

CHAPTER 9: WHEN OTHERS DON'T UNDERSTAND RETROACTIVE JEALOUSY

At the time of writing this book, Retroactive Jealousy seems to be somewhat of an overlooked and relatively unheard of condition. There are, however, some fantastic sources to use for recovery During most of my RJ rampant years, anything I tried to look up on the subject induced many painful triggers and did not help me. Ultimately searching online did cure my RJ in the end, so the triggers were well worth it. If you are searching online for answers and are often triggered then I recommend you soldier on. The triggers are painful but will not kill you. Focus on your conscious presence and allow the triggers to be. As mentioned at the beginning of this book, use the triggers to your advantage. They are challenges tailor-made for you, telling you to grow.

Your RJ may feel completely reasonable and understandable to you, but do not expect your friends, family or acquaintances to get it. They likely will not. They will offer unhelpful feedback such as "well everyone has done something with someone" or "why would you even think about your girlfriend's/boyfriend's past?". This will perhaps bring about fleeting relief at best. But don't fret. You do not need them to understand. The only thing that matters is your own personal recovery and this can only happen from the inside. No amount of external advice from someone that does not understand is likely to bring about your transformation. Following the advice and taking action on the areas discussed in this book and other good sources will ultimately bring about your transformation. My friends and family all looked at me as though I was crazy when I would mention to them that was so distraught over my partners past. Remember, if they have not suffered with RJ themselves, then they will simply never fully understand. Just go with the understanding that they are doing their best with the information and resources that they have available to them.

You will likely feel compelled to talk about RJ regularly to friends and family. This is due to the obsessive-compulsive nature of RJ. It will try to capture your mind's attention as frequently as possible. Try to avoid this cunning RJ trap if possible. It will often end in more triggers and more mind food for your RJ to gobble up and sustain itself with. The trick to success lies in abandoning all RJ thoughts as they appear. This starves RJ and shrinks its power. When I was suffering with RJ, I often felt as if a demon was screaming in my face for attention all day and night. As I progressed with my trigger and presence work, the demon would shrink and shrink as it had no food to feed on and grow. I was no longer serving up delicious all you can eat dishes of trigger cooked, jealousy garnished intrusive thoughts on a silver platter. Eventually, the demon shrunk so much that it became more like a leprechaun trying to stamp on my toe for attention. I soon after stamped on this leprechaun and was prized with the proverbial pot of gold; my cured RJ and all of its benefits. RJ's recovery bought about my spiritual awakening, enhanced mental/physical strength, a new work ethic, and a more loving and emotionally intelligent me.

Getting you to discuss RJ with loved ones is one of the cunning tricks it often pulls to get more mind food. The more you talk about RJ, the more power you give it. You becoming tiresome of the pain will push you to seek relief in many areas. Try to be strong and avoid discussing RJ as much as possible outside of therapy sessions or other past RJ sufferers. This doesn't mean you shouldn't seek solace from loved ones during a painful time. But you must simply remain aware of RJ's cunning tricks and traps to get you to feed it. You may even start to laugh at how silly its efforts become as you practice becoming aware of RJ's methods. You may also even be impressed with RJ's chess master like intellect. Just remember that this intellect is you. You cannot outsmart it because it is you. But if your RJ is that cunning and clever, then so are you, because it is, in fact, your own mind activity. Imagine a world where that cunning intellect can be put to good constructive use! Take a few moments and imagine what you could accomplish when you transform RJ's genius, energy, and relentlessness into a new positive, creative outlet. You will be an unstoppable force for good once this painful energy is transformed into life-affirming power. I believe that the true cause of RJ is the universes way to force you to evolve and grow. Looking at it in this way, your RJ becomes a gift-wrapped present from the heavens.

In short, do not worry about whether your loved ones, partner or friends understand Retroactive Jealousy. They don't need to. The answer to the cure lies deep within you. You have the power to unleash your healing life-force and work towards permanent, positive change.

✤ 10 ✤

CHAPTER 10: CLEARING UP THE WRECKAGE

SAYING SORRY

An important part of your journey after overcoming RJ is forgiving yourself for any damage you may have caused and for any actions that you may now regret. This does not mean that you don't accept full responsibility for your past actions. It means that you are ready for change and have eliminated your destructive patterns. You could have only acted as your consciousness allowed and at that time your consciousness was in a trigger induced trance-like state. Your being afflicted with RJ was/is not your fault, but it is your responsibly to put right any wrongdoings on your part. You must forgive yourself. You must also apologize to your partner and others for any insensitive things you may have said or done to those caught in your painful outbursts. But make sure to apologize when you are at a point when you will not be triggered again. You may cause excess unnecessary turmoil if you are not ready and your attempts to apologize are thwarted by additional triggers. We must do the hard internal work to eliminate triggers first before embarking on our forgiveness journey. You may feel a new sense of positive energy once you have apologized to those you have hurt. This is due to the closure you and those affected will gain and it will give you the added excitement of starting fresh and turning over a new leaf. Being forgiven by those you have hurt is a powerful transformative gift you can fully utilize in your own healing process. Later in life, you will be glad that you have taken the time to repair these friendships/relationships and those you have apologized to will often be grateful too. No one likes to have unresolved toxic energy residing anywhere near their aura or psyche, conscious or unconscious.

THOSE WHO DO NOT ACCEPT FORGIVENESS

There may be certain friends/partners of family members that will not accept your apologies depending on how extreme your particular struggle with RJ got, how intense your outbursts or how venomous your choice of words. This is their choice and you must respect their decision and personal healing time. But do not fret. Time can heal all wounds and eventually this important person will see your transformation with their own eyes if you allow such an opportunity. Once you let go of the steering wheel and realize that you cannot change others' opinions of you, you will leave plenty of space to give the unforgiving person time without trying to control or manipulate their verdict of you. This does not mean say sorry and disappear. It just means to allow them plenty of time and space without trying to control their feelings about you after you have made your initial apology. Periodically check in on them as long as they have not overtly affirmed otherwise. You may find over time that their efforts to cut you out and hold a grudge are more tiresome than actually giving you another chance. This can lead to their gradual acceptance of you and your reappearance in their life. On the other hand, if they portray strongly that they do not want to see you again and the damage caused is just too much, then you must accept their decision fully and take it as a life lesson and signal that you must defeat RJ fully and permanently so that you will not lose more important people during your life due to unresolved demons. Letting go and moving on can be agonizing, especially when you know you cannot right a wrong an older version of yourself is responsible for. However, you must use this pain as a fire to fuel the creation of the greatest future version of yourself. You can become this version today by making a stand and taking the right choice, right now. You must also forgive yourself. The most important relationship you will ever have is the relationship with yourself. You are the only person you will not lose throughout your lifetime. Let's make sure you are in a state of peace and forgiveness for as many of your days as possible.

❧ 11 ❧
CHAPTER 11: LIFE AFTER RETROACTIVE JEALOUSY

Congratulations! If you have made it this far then you have likely absorbed lots of helpful information and practices and are well on your way to forgetting RJ for good. If you do not feel like you are gradually ridding yourself of RJ then do not despair as you will likely need to revisit sections of this book and re-read them while implementing the actions necessary to succeed. It is imperative that you take action on the exercises and practices mentioned throughout the book, otherwise, your progress may not be powered with the boost it needs to fast-track your recovery. The affirmations are presented to you to reprogram your subconscious mind. This will be one of the most transformative tools in changing the way you look at yourself. Programming the subconscious mind has the potential to improve every area of your life. It is also extremely important that you learn to deal with triggers. You must remain focussed and present when struck by a trigger and you must not get emotionally attached to them. Let them fade away in the fleeting, whizzing highway that is your train of thought.

You will likely encounter days where you feel overwhelmed by your RJ and its accompanying triggers. You may feel as though you have not made progress and are down on yourself because you are triggered again. Do not despair, as these days are opportunities to become even stronger and more proficient at dealing with triggers. Remember, if you can't feel it then you can't heal it. Be grateful for these kinds of slump days as they are pulling out the remaining RJ from your being. Power through these days as if you are cleansing yourself fully of any remnants of RJ. You may continue through your life being triggered from time to time, but just remember what I mentioned at the beginning of this book; I am 100% trigger free and suffer from RJ no more. No remnants remain and I could be (and have been) in the same room as a partner's ex and feel absolutely no trace of RJ. I believe in time and with much work that this can be possible for you too and all sufferers of RJ.

THE UNIVERSE TESTING YOU

You may find yourself encountering new situations that will challenge you and your new coping skills to boundaries never before reached. As you become stronger, the challenges the universe will offer you may increase in difficulty before you have fully transformed your RJ. This is the universes way of telling you that there is still work to be done! I will explain with an example that the universe presented to me.

In the midst of my RJ, I was suffering relentlessly and was then piling this hurt onto my partner, cunningly trying to pull information about her past from her. Whenever she even mentioned a male friend, I would immediately interrogate her and try to find out if anything had happened between them. I found out that she was involved intimately with one particular friend. The pain was excruciating. As your subconscious mind and body can't tell the difference between a thought and a real situation, This felt like I was being cheated on in real-time, which was not the case. Days passed and I was embarking on a new career endeavor and traveling the country. As I was discussing the crew members for the trip with a colleague, I discovered that I would be traveling the country by bus with none other than my aforementioned partner's ex-lover. "What are the odds!?" I miserably uttered to myself. Out of all the guys in the entire city, I ended up with my partner's ex. (I would later realize that my being placed in this predicament against unbelievable odds was the universes way of telling me I had much work left to do.) This was my worst nightmare come true, I was sharing a bus with someone my partner had been intimate with for some time in the past. His name was Tim. The fact that I would be in close quarters with Tim for an extended time almost ended my relationship with my partner right then and there. I passively aggressively passed on the information of the trip and its participants to my partner and she was overwhelmed with dread. She knew what she was in store for. Fast forward several days into the trip, I had managed to subdue my urges to ask cunning questions to my new colleague that would provide me with plenty of RJ food right from the source. I was surprised and proud of myself, although the true purpose of subduing my urges was to not embarrass myself and present myself to my peers as insecure. As I got to know Tim, I realized that he was not this macho, rough and tough, powerful, superior man that I had conjured up in my imagination. I saw on a personal basis that he was just a human being, with the same fears, insecurities, and hangups that we all seem to possess at one stage or another. It gave me tangible experience that my imagination and RJ thoughts were not based on reality. The images portrayed to me by my mind were apparitions of my own insecurity, they were not sprouted from truth. If my RJ images were this far off in this case, then how false were my assumptions of my partner's other exes and intimate encounters? I began to see the falsehood of RJ's image conjuring and started to see through the games of my own mind. There was a glaring hole in all of RJ's apparitions, one torn by tangibly triggered logic and real-life gathered information. This self-awareness was a powerful contributor to my transformation of RJ. Tim was respectful, kind and likable. He was quiet, relatively insecure himself (a thought that had never crossed my RJ infected mind) and helpful with work efforts. He was an avid gym-goer, which initially inflamed my RJ to heated temperatures and caused my insecurity much panic. I was not a gym-goer, and my body was not in particularly impressive shape. I had found a point of comparison for my RJ to latch on to. Instead of becoming hopelessly lost in despair, I chose to accompany Tim to a gym while on the road. He showed me his work out routine, how long he spent on cardio, what weight exercises he did and so on. I started incorporating these workouts into my daily life and began to feel a new sense of enjoyment I had not felt in years. The physical exercise was releasing endorphins and changing my mood and energy for the better. Over time, Tim and I became friends and I become an avid gymgoer myself. By the end of the work trip, I had discovered so much about myself, the falsities of my RJ and about compassion and empathy. I would no longer look at my partner's exes as monstrous threats, but simply as human beings, with the same core needs and desires as all of us. This was massively life-altering. I had learned so much about working out from Tim that I go to the gym everyday still to this day. This fact alone, I would not change for the world as physical fitness is now a huge part of my life. I was forced to spend several weeks coping with triggers that were physically right in front of my face, this was the ultimate challenge, but I came through the other side unscathed and my relationship with Sarah intact, with only a few RJ triggered hiccups along the way. My physical fitness and mental state was on the rise dramatically. Soon after the trip, I realized that being put into that situation against unbelievable odds was one of the greatest things that could have ever happened to me. If I could get through what I initially perceived as a nightmare situation, then I could get through anything that RJ could throw at me. I thank the universe for placing me in that situation. If you find yourself in a similar situation where your RJ coping skills are tested to all ends, then simply smile, and say thank you to the universe. Thank you for giving me exactly what I need, when I need it, no matter how painful. And thank you for showing me that there is still more work to be done! Say yes to the universe. Say yes to the intelligent flow of life that we cannot begin to comprehend. Saying yes to the intelligent life flow of the universe is one of your greatest resources. It is all within you.

IN CLOSING

I truly hope that you, the reader are positively inspired by this book to complete your RJ work and transform your pain into power. This transformation will bring about a wonderful change in every area of your life. You will have access to so many more life possibilities that you were previously blocked from due to your emotional state. Remember, no matter how hard it may seem, no matter how much you feel like giving up into a pit of despair, no matter how impossible healing my seem, I write this book to you as an ex RJ sufferer that is 100% cured. The same is possible for you. The key to your progress and healing is in your hands. Own it fully and take control! Do not waste any more of your life confined to the nightmarish symptoms of your insecurity. It is time to thrive and live your life! Enjoy every day, enjoy every second. Be here now and breathe in the beauty that is all around you. You are a powerful force for good. I believe in you. Now you must believe in yourself. Godspeed!

YOUR FEEDBACK IS VALUED

From the bottom of my heart, thank you for reading my book. I truly hope that it helps you heal from Retroactive Jealousy and live a more empowered and happy life. If it does help you, then I'd like to ask you for a favor. Would you be kind enough to leave a review for this book on Amazon? It'd be greatly appreciated and will likely impact the lives of other Retroactive Jealousy sufferers across the globe, giving them hope and healing.

They are suffering like you and I have and we can help them move past this together.

I read every review I receive and each one helps me to become a more knowledgeable and compassionate writer to serve you better.

Thank you and good luck,
    Ryder Winchester

Please go here to leave a review: viewbook.at/retroactive-jealousy

Milton Keynes UK
Ingram Content Group UK Ltd.
UKHW022032151223
434483UK00005B/89